The
Rhyming Princess

Once upon a time, there
was a princess named Selina,
who always spoke in rhyme.
Her family loved her,
but they found this
very annoying.

When her family wished her good morning at breakfast, she said, *"Please speak clearly. Do not mutter! Father, could you pass the butter?"*

"Why can't you talk properly, like other people?" asked her sister Amelia.

Selina said, *"To talk this way is right for me. Now why is that so hard to see?"*

"You're just showing off," said Amelia, with a toss of her head.

"That's enough!"
cried their father,
the king. He was
so annoyed that
his crown slipped
down over one eye.
"I won't have this
arguing at breakfast!
Just eat without
ANY talking,
rhyming or
not rhyming!"

7

When the two princesses had left the breakfast table, the queen asked the king, "What shall we do about Selina? She can't go through life talking in rhyme."

"We will have to do something," sighed the king. "People will laugh at her. After all, she *is* a princess!"

So the king and queen
sent for the best doctors
in the whole world.
The doctors asked Selina
to open her mouth.

They peered down her throat. They X-rayed her and took her temperature. But they couldn't find ANYTHING wrong with her!

Selina became very angry.
"*If rhymes don't please
the queen and king,
I'll never say another thing!*"

And she refused to speak
from that day onward.

Selina's family missed her rhyming speech. The king and queen wished they had left things as they were. They decided to send messengers far and wide, asking if anyone knew how to solve the problem.

15

The days passed, but still
Selina refused to talk.
Then, one day, a young
man arrived at the palace
and asked to speak
to Princess Selina.

"I don't think so!" shouted
the king. "She hasn't spoken
to ANYONE for AGES!
Why would she speak
to you?"

But he sent for the princess.

16

When Selina came into
the room, the young man
began to speak
to her in rhyme!

"Princess, I heard
of you one day
in Rhyming Kingdom,
far away.
There, we all love
rhyming, too.
In fact, we all speak
just like you!"

19

Princess Selina began
to smile, and her eyes
sparkled.

The young man went on:
"*In Rhyming Kingdom,
if you choose,
you can make a speech
or read the news.
If you decide
to come with me,
you can rhyme all day
quite happily!*"

Princess Selina's smile
became a laugh.
Then she spoke for
the first time in weeks.

"May I go,
dear family?
This Rhyming Kingdom
is for me!
You can visit,
Father, Mother.
Bring my sister
and my brother!"

22

So they all visited
the Rhyming Kingdom.
The king and queen agreed
that Selina could stay.
*And in that land
of rhyme and laughter,
she lived happily ever after!*